Woodland Chic

Metal Clay Jewelry as Nature Intended

by Patrik Kusek

"Art is born of the observation and investigation of nature."
~Cicero (106 BC - 43 BC)

ISBN 978-1-105-21520-9

First Edition
Published by Patrik Kusek, Wallop Design Group Inc. and Patrik's
Studio, Fairfield, CA 94533

{ CONTENTS }

{ INTRODUCTION }

I've

seen it many times. I've read it in everything
from novels to how-to books. It seems to be a cliché, a
standard idiom to include. A sort of prerequisite to authordom.
But the term "labor of love" seems to sum up the truth in a way no other
phrase can. As a first time author, I have a need to ponder each and every project
this book would offer. Is this an interesting enough project? Does it show something
new? Does it represent my aesthetic? I need my artistic vision to come through. I need
my sense of design to tell a story not only through its words, but through my sense of artistry.
My prior career as an art director haunts me this way. My experience as a fashion stylist demands
it. But with my creative muses tugging in so many directions, it can get complicated. Doubts start
to surface; "Is this project really good enough for my readers?" "Have I seen this project before?"
"What am I doing!?" So as projects are revised and revised again, and layouts are designed and
refined, the book title has changed to represent the new concepts presented and the cover design
has changed as well. Yes, you can judge this book by its cover...at least I hope so. The passion, the
art, the vision. Along the way, one of the many lessons learned while writing this book is a new
respect for the publishing world. Plus, I learned that although I have the capability to
design and produce a book like this, I'd much rather have someone do it for me. The "director" part of my art director past rears his micromanaging head, but for all the time and
effort spent on the details and minutia, I'm thrilled to present you with "Woodland
Chic." Everything in this book is my vision: from concept to creation. I conceived it,
designed the layouts, chose the type, took the photos for and assembled all of the
collages, designed the projects, and wrote the step-by-step instructions and
in most cases (unless noted) took the photos as well. So it seems some-
how not right that I must rely on the aforementioned cliché to
help express my feelings of the whole process. My fellow
artist.......please enjoy this book, because
indeed it was a labor of love.

{ HOW TO USE THIS BOOK }

Observe, construct, understand, repeat. Retain. My approach to learning is similar to my approach to teaching: It's an organic but methodical one, a fine balance of providing information in a clear concise manner and providing latitude for creative absorption of the process. When I teach a PMC Certification workshop for Rio Grande, I will challenge my students to not only emulate the process, but look for other practical uses for the techniques learned. *The dreaded tetrahedron* is a great example of this. This project requires the ability to see razor sharp edges, a steady hand and lots of patience. Students will often say that while the technique was interesting, they probably would never make a tetrahedron again. But when challenged as to how they might "apply" the new technique to other projects, the list grows: dimensional shadow boxes, hollow beads, lockets, and the list goes on. This book was designed with this kind of learning in mind, not only providing a step-by-step process, but also providing practical challenges to use the knowledge provided. This is done by presenting a series of "design challenges." These challenges are presented as photos of completed projects with a question attached. When you think you have solved the question, follow the link to my website to find the answer.

Similarly there are links for technique videos. Visit the link indicated to hear my description of either the process or different technique. Also, for the sake of brevity, I've shortened the step-by-step directions to take out repetitive information. For instance, instead of detailing out how to apply liver of sulfur for every project, I'll simply say "add LOS" or "finish in the usual manner." Find directions in Chapter 5: Foundations and on the Woodland Chic website. In addition, projects are written using PMC brand metal clay. Art Clay Silver or any other brand metal clay can easily be substituted for any project. There are also easy to identify icons which show the level of difficulty: **[B]** for beginner, **[I]** for intermediate and **[A]** for advanced. I've included this because some designs seem quite simple, however a beginner could be technically challenged. Other projects seem complex but are actually easy. My hope is that whatever level you are at currently, you will learn from these projects, then use the techniques for your own beautiful and unique creations.

Go forth and create, because *"Passion Fuels Creativity."*

No. 1

"When I learn something new – and it happens every day – I feel a little more at home in this universe, a little more comfortable in the nest."
~Bill Moyers

EARRINGS
{ TWIGS AND NESTS }

TREES, branches, twigs…the organic nature of these items form the structure for most of the plant life that graces our world. You'll see this structure not only in the forest but in the sea as well. With different methods of how to make twigs, you'll have the versatility to adapt the design to your own creations.

[1]

MATERIALS

PMC+ (or PMC3) 28 grams
2 Fine Silver Eyelets 1.6mm
Pro Polish polishing squares
Liver of Sulfur
Earring Wires

TOOLS

Basic Metal Clay Tool Kit
Brass Brush
Tweezers
Rubber Tipped Clay Shaper
Needle Tool
Dockyard Carving Tool
  V-Gouge 2mm
Teflon Sheet
Snake Roller

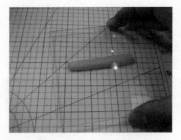

1 Using a piece of plexiglass or a snake roller, roll two snakes approximately 2.5" long. This will become the main branch.

2 Cut the snakes using a sharp craft knife. Use a rolling motion to cut the snake so as not to smash the snake while cutting it.

3 Next insert the stem of a 1.6mm fine silver eyelet into the snake.

4 The stem should be buried deep into the branch so that the round part of the eyelet is just below the surface.

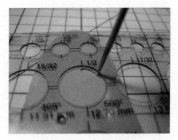

5 Next roll some clay 3 cards thick. Using an awl or pin tool cut a 1/2" circle using a circle template as a guide.

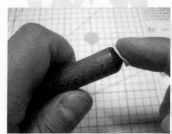

6 Place the wet clay circle onto a small lubricated doming tool. In this example the end of a Kemper pin tool was used.

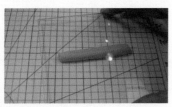

✱ To see a video on how to roll a snake, visit www.woodlandchic.net/snakes

7 Using a bent-tipped dental tool or a small wire bent into an "L" shape, press a texture into the wet clay. The texture should follow the shape of the nest simulating the twigs. Repeat for the other earring. Set aside to dry.

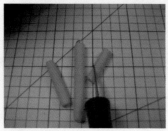

8 Next, roll out two snakes approximately 2" long. Make this snake a little narrower in thickness than the main branch. Set aside to dry. After drying cut them into four pieces. Each piece should be a different length. Cut one end of the branches at a 45 degree angle.

9 Using a 2mm size V-shaped gouge, gently carve short and long random lines into the dried branch. This will add texture to simulate bark.

10 The carved lines should be of varying depths, lengths and thicknesses. The carved lines should be parallel but slightly mis-aligned to give a more organic feel to the bark.

11 Take a superfine grade sanding sponge and bend it in half. The folded edge will be rounded. Use the rounded edge of the sponge to sand a concave shape into the end of the branch.

12 Attach the side branch to the center branch using water and slip.

13 Make egg shapes by rolling a small amount of clay into a ball. Gently press while rolling one end of the ball to create the egg shape. Set aside to dry.

14 To create the vine, roll out a length of clay a little longer than the length of the branch. Taper the ends of the vine. Wrap the branch with the vine and secure using water.

15 Attach the eggs to the nest and attach the nest to the crotch of the branch using water and slip.

16 Secure all components by using water and slip. Set aside to dry. Do a final check and sand any rough areas. Fire according to manufacturer's instructions and finish in the usual manner.

TECHNIQUE
{ 3 Ways to Make Twigs & Branches }

Enjoy the process of experimenting. When I start a project I usually think I know how I will construct a piece. However, sometimes it's not always the most efficient or unique way. I have to remind myself to explore the options. I always do this with the design of my pieces, but in construction I'm constantly having to fight the urge to dive right in and start making. Below are 3 different ways to make twigs and branches.

Method 1 - Carve

1 Rollout a clay snake to the desired length and about 1/4" thick. Pinch the snake and bend at an angle. Repeat pinching and bending, changing angles each time. Set snake aside to dry.

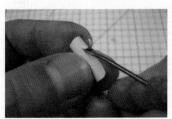

2 Using a 1.5mm V-Shaped gouge carve short lines in the snake. Make each line a different length and at slightly different angles. Repeat until the entire branch is carved. Smooth the cuts with a slightly damp brush in a scrubbing motion.

Method 2 - Wire Brush

1 Rollout a clay snake to the desired length and about 1/4" thick. Pinch the snake and bend at an angle. Repeat pinching and bending, changing angles each time.

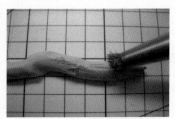

2 Use a brass pen brush to scratch a wood grain pattern into the wet branch. Then use the tip of a mechanical pencil to create a knot hole.

Method 3 - Molds

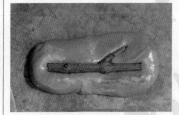

1 Mix two part mold compound and insert twig into the compound. Make sure not to press too deep to avoid piercing the bottom of the compound. Let cure according to manufacturer's instructions. Remove the twig.

2 Press clay into the mold. Remove any excess clay from the edge of the mold. Set aside to dry before removing the branch. Sand any excess clay that has gone over the edges.

{ DELICATE BRANCHES }

TO CREATE THESE DELICATE BRANCHES I used metal clay that comes in a syringe. This type of clay is more viscous than the lump clay form. You can cut the tip of the syringe to get different sized openings. I usually have a couple of different sized tips around my work bench within easy reach. Plus, the combination of resin and tissue paper create a wonderful transparent stained glass effect.

[I]

MATERIALS

PMC+ (or PMC3) 18 grams
PMC+ or PMC3 Syringe
Pro Polish polishing squares
Liver of Sulfur
Tissue Paper
2 Part Epoxy Resin

TOOLS

Basic Metal Clay Tool Kit
Brass Brush
Scissors
Rubber Tipped Clay Shaper
Needle Tool or Sharp
  Dental Tool
Teflon Sheet
Shield Shaped Template
Texture Plate

* For tips on using 2 part resin, visit www.woodlandchic.com/resin

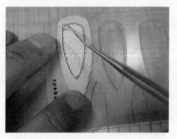

1 Roll out a lump of clay 3 cards thick. Using the shield shaped template, cut out a large shape, and with a smaller size template cut out a window. Set aside to dry. Drill a hole for the ear wire. Refine the edges with sand paper.

2 Using a Sharpie marker and template, draw the smaller shield shape, then draw a tree silhouette inside the shield. Place the drawing under a Teflon sheet. Use it as a guide to build the rest of the earrings.

3 Using a syringe tip with a larger opening, extrude the main branch. Use a start-and-stop motion. Start the branch, then stop and, without lifting the syringe, change the direction of the branch. Repeat until the main branch is connected to the top and bottom of the shield.

4 Using a smaller syringe tip create branches by connecting the main branch to the inside edge of the shield and over the front. Using a pin tool, split the tip of the branch into smaller branches. Set aside to dry. Refine the edges with sanding sponges. Fire and finish as usual.

5 Mix up two part resin and brush it over tissue paper on a Teflon sheet.

6 Place the finished earring on top of the resin. Add more resin to fill the inside of the earrings. The edges should be completely sealed with resin. Set aside to dry completely. When dry, approximately 24 hours, trim the edges with scissors.

{ MINIATURE PEDESTAL VESSEL }

MATERIALS

PMC+ (or PMC3) 28 grams

Aura 22

TOOLS

Basic Metal Clay Tool Kit

Brass Brush

Rubber Tipped Clay Shaper

Craft Knife

Needle Tool or Sharp
  Dental Tool

Small brass teardrop shaped cutter

Ping Pong Ball

Circle Template

400 grit emery paper

Brush for Aura 22

Butane Torch

Solderite Pad

MY STUDENT'S CREATIVITY never ceases to amaze me. This project was inspired by a design that a student made during one of my workshops at The Ranch Center for Arts and Craft in Snohomish, WA. While initially designed as a salt cellar, this design can be modified for a variety of different uses by changing the size or shape of the vessel.

1 Create the leaves. Roll out clay 2 cards thick. Using a teardrop shaped cutter, cut out approximately 15 teardrop shapes.

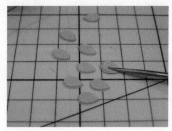

2 Using a pin tool gently make an impression into the teardrop shape. Be careful not to cut all of the way through.

3 Alternatively make the indentation while holding the shape on a finger tip instead of the table. Set aside to dry and sand the edges to refine.

4 Roll out a lump of clay 4 cards thick. Using a 1" circle template and pin tool, cut out a circle. If you want to add a texture be sure to do it while you roll out the clay.

5 Shape the circle over a lubricated ping-pong ball. Set aside to dry.

6 Using the 400 grit emery paper, sand the edge flat.

7 Check the edge to be sure it comes to a clean sharp bevel.

8 Roll out some clay 2 cards thick. Use a brass or steel brush to make a texture in the clay.

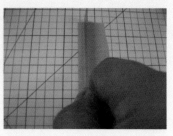

9 Using a tissue blade cut several strips of clay approx 1" long in two different widths: 1/4" wide and 1/8" wide.

10 Attach the thicker pieces first using water, then attach the thinner ones. Be sure to cut the thinner pieces at an angle to fit to the wider branch.

11 Next attach the leaf shapes to the branches using water.

12 Make the pedestal base by creating a half dome shape in the same manner as step 4-7. Be sure to use a 1/2" or 3/4" circle shape. Attach the smaller dome to the top dome using water and slip. Dry, sand and fire. Cool the piece.

13 Determine where the gold will be applied. Apply a thin coating of slip to any areas where gold is wanted. Dry.

14 Apply the Aura 22 to the areas painted with slip. Apply 2 to 3 coats of Aura 22. Use a torch to fire the Aura 22. Apply LOS and finish as usual.

© *Photography by Drew Davidson*

WHAT TECHNIQUES WOULD YOU USE TO CREATE THIS PROJECT?
The materials are PMC, PMC Syringe and Fine Silver Eyelets.
Visit WWW.WOODLANDCHIC.NET/GARDENGATE to find the answer.

No. 2

"*There is always music amongst the trees in the garden, but our hearts must be very quiet to hear it.*"

~*Minnie Aumonier*

{ Faux Bois }

BRONZE OR COPPER CUFF
{ FAUX BOIS CUFF }

THE FRENCH TERM FAUX BOIS means "False Wood." First used in outdoor furniture in the 1800's, the style was popularized in the 1920's and is still used widely today in metal furniture, stationery, rugs and jewelry. This cuff takes its cue from the traditional method of 200 years ago by using carving to impart the grain-like texture of the wood.

MATERIALS

200 grams of BronzClay or CopprClay
White Carbon paper
Wooden Bracelet Mandrel
Plastic Wrap
Pen

TOOLS

Basic Metal Clay Tool Kit
3M Sanding Sponges
Dockyard Carving Tool
* U-Gouge 2mm*

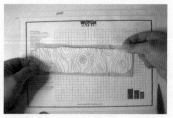

1 Download the Faux Bois template at www.woodlandchic.net/cufftemplate. Print out the template and cut out the cuff shape. Wrap a wooden bracelet mandrel with plastic wrap. Roll out a slab of BronzClay or CopprClay 6 to 8 cards thick. Lay the paper template on top of the clay and cut out the shape using a needle tool.

2 Wrap the clay around the mandrel and dry. Lay the carbon paper on top of the dried clay. Lay the template on top of the carbon paper. Trace the wood grain pattern with a pencil. The carbon paper will transfer the pattern to the dried clay.

3 Using a 2 mm U-shaped gouge, gently carve out the texture.

4 Carve all the way to the edges.

5 Sand the edges with sanding sponges until smooth.

6 With a slightly damp brush, use a scrubbing motion to smooth any rough spots. The brush should be slightly damp and not too wet. Dry, fire and finish as usual.

As an alternative to clay, try a faux bois carving technique on polymer clay or another material. For this piece I carved into antique bakelite.

Opposite page

Untitled
1 1/2" x 1 1/2"
Antique resin shield
Fine Silver
22K Gold

© *Photography by Abbey Johnston*

"Desire"
1 1/2" x 2 1/4"
Antique Bakelite
Fine Silver
Antique Lava Cameo
Copper
Freshwater Pearl
Tourmaline

© *Photography by Abbey Johnston*

What techniques would you use to create this project?
The materials are BronzClay and CopprClay.
Visit www.woodlandchic.net/bimetalcuff to find the answer.

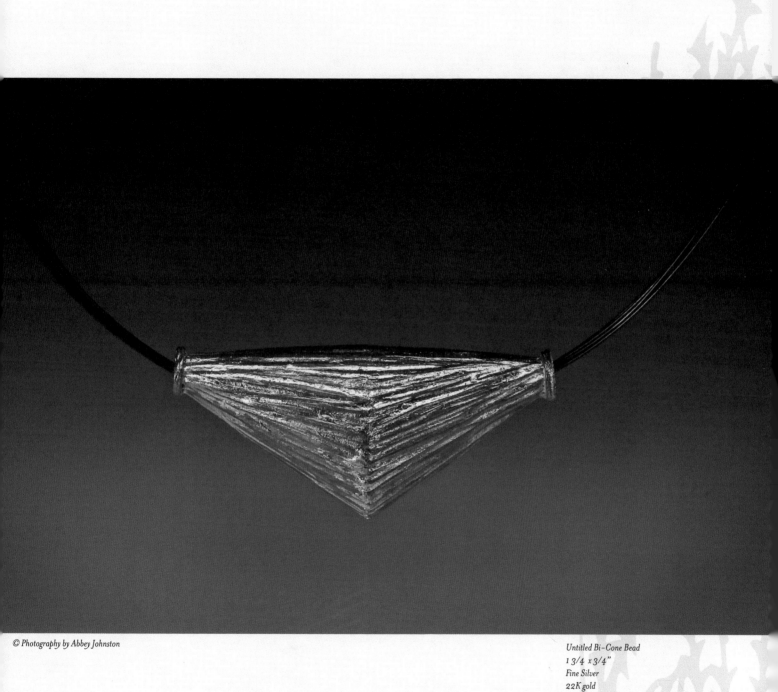

Untitled Bi-Cone Bead
1 3/4 x 3/4"
Fine Silver
22K gold

NECKLACE
{ LUCKY BAMBOO PENDANT }

BAMBOO is the most prevalent building material on earth. It is renewable because of its fast growth. Although technically a grass, the bamboo forests of Japan would rival the California redwoods in their beauty. This project uses a variety of techniques seen in other projects and introduces the use of PMC Sheet.

[1]

MATERIALS

18 grams PMC+ or PMC3
PMC Syringe
PMC Sheet

TOOLS

Basic Metal Clay Tool Kit
Dockyard Carving Tool
  U-Gouge 1.5mm
Craft Knife
Texture Plate
Circle Template

1 Roll out the clay to a thickness of 4 cards. Using a circle template and pin tool, cut out a circle 1 3/8" large.

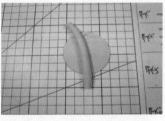

2 Using a small straw cut a hole for the jump ring. Next, roll out a snake approximately 2" long and 1/4" wide. Set both items aside to dry.

3 Mark the snake with a pencil at 1/2" intervals. Using the gouge, carve short lines between the marks.

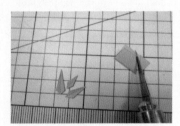

4 Cut out the leaf shapes from PMC Sheet. Make each leaf a different size.

5 Connect the bamboo to the pendant using some water and slip. Use a pencil to mark where the branches will be. Check the shape of the branch by laying the leaves on the pendant. Make any adjustments to the design if necessary. Make the branches using metal clay syringe.

6 Connect the leaves to the pendant by pressing the leaf into the wet branch. To make the center vein of the leaf press a pin tool into the leaf hard enough to make a mark. Repeat with other leaves. Fire and finish as usual.

No. 3

"*The greatest artist has no conception which a single block of white marble does not potentially contain within its mass, but only a hand obedient to the mind can penetrate to this image.*"
~Michelangelo

{ 2 PART MOLD COMPOUND }

DETAILS COME TO LIFE. A variety of different materials can be used to make textures and molds; however, 2 part silicone mold compound can yield stunning results with relative ease. Most manufacturers' instructions are similar. The compound usually comes in two containers, the hardening agent and the silicone compound. The process is very simple: Gently knead equal parts of the two compounds together until the mixture is one consistent color. Incorporate the two compounds quickly as most compounds will start to cure within a couple of minutes. This is known as the "pot life" or "working time." Next, place the object you would like to mold inside the compound and set aside to cure. Do not remove the object until the compound has cured. Alternatively, to make a texture plate, you can roll out the compound using playing cards as risers, then press the texture onto the compound and re-roll. Set aside to cure. Each manufacturer has different working times and cure times, so refer to manufacturer's instructions for details. For a video on making molds and textures using 2 part silicone mold compound, visit www.woodlandchic.net/moldcompound

PENDANT
{ SHADOW BOX PENDANT }

CAPTURE, contain, preserve. This simple shadow box was inspired by a recent trip to Washington. Seattle is just a short plane flight from the San Francisco Bay area, but it has dramatically different types of mountains. In that vein, shadow box shapes themselves are as versatile as the contents they can hold, from metal clay objects to found objects captured in resin. Capture the moment!

[A]

MATERIALS

28 grams PMC+ or PMC3
Aura 22
2 Part Mold Compound
Small branch
Small Leaves

TOOLS

Basic Metal Clay Tool Kit
Dockyard Carving Tool
  U-Gouge 2mm

1 Roll out a piece of clay 4 cards thick, leaving a rough edge. The piece should be approximately 2" x 4".

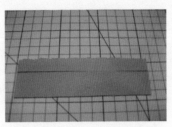

2 Cut a strip around 1/2" wide and 3 1/2" long. These will be used to make the sides of the shadowbox.

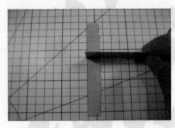

3 Cut 2 strips approx 1 1/4" long and 2 strips 3/4" long.

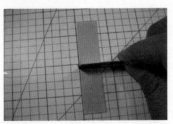

4 Using the remainder of the clay, cut the back of the shadowbox. The piece should be 1 1/2" x 1".

5 Press clay into a branch mold. Remove any excess clay that exceeds the size of the mold. {See page 32 for mold making.} Set aside to dry.

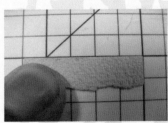

6 Use an emery file and the grid to square up 3 of the sides leaving the rough side as-is.

7 Bevel the left and right edges of all the shadowbox panels by sanding the edge at a 45 degree angle against an emery board.

8 Using water and slip join the top and right side to form an "L" shape. Use the edge of a ruler or spacer to keep the pieces to a right angle. Repeat for the bottom and left pieces. Set aside to dry.

9 Next join the halves using water and slip to complete the frame of the box.

10 Using syringe or paste, reinforce the inside corners of the box. Set aside to dry.

11 Using a new craft knife, bevel the inside edges of the box by scraping. Make sure to bevel each of the four edges. Leave the front edge of the box natural.

12 Next, trace the shape of the frame onto the dried piece of 1 1/2" by 1" clay. This will be the back of the shadowbox.

13 Bevel the inside edges of the back of the box. Be sure to do several test fits along the way. It's better to take off a little at a time than risk removing too much.

14 Roll out a piece of clay 2 cards thick that is larger than the size of the box. Dry to *leather hard*. When dry, gently rip the top 1/3 of the piece. Make the tear in the shape of a mountain range.

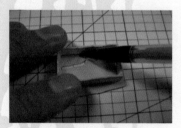

15 Lay the torn pieces side by side leaving a gap. Position the frame over the mountain range pieces. Use a mechanical pencil to mark the shape of the inside of the box. Cut the pieces to fit.

16 Use scrap pieces of clay that have been rolled out to 4 cards thick to raise the mountain shape off the surface of the back of the box.

17 Repeat the process with the second half of the mountain range. Set aside to dry. Do a test fit and shape the sides accordingly.

18 Attach the back of the box using water and slip. Set aside to dry.

19 Roll out a small snake 2mm to 3mm thick. Gently shape the snake over a small straw making a U-shape. Set aside to dry.

20 Cut the ends even using a craft knife.

21 Join the "U" shape to the bottom of the box using water and slip.

22 Make a mold of a small fern leaf. Press the clay into the mold.

23 Lift up the clay to check the impression. Set aside to dry.

24 Using a craft knife, gently carve the excess clay to form the shape of the leaf.

25 Use the branch from step 5 and carve any excess material using a craft knife. Sand the edge if necessary.

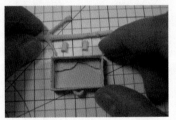

26 To make the posts use extra parts of the branch or roll out snakes and dry. Join the top branch to the posts and top of the box. Set aside to dry. Do any last detail sanding.

27 Use vermiculite to support the box and branch while firing. Vermiculite will prevent the box and branch from slumping during the firing process.

28 Use Aura 22 to paint the background and sun. Add at least 2 coats. {For more details on using Aura 22, see the Adding Gold link on page 58.} Finish as usual.

Untitled Shadowbox
2" x 2"
Fine Silver

Shadow boxes are a great option because of the variety of materials that can be incorporated into the design. Here, the seashore theme provided wonderful imagery from which to pull.

Tip: If your original objects are too large to fit into the shadow box, make a mold and use PMC Original to make the component. Fire the component. The high shrinkage of PMC Original will make the piece smaller. You can then attach this piece to a pre-fired shadowbox.

You can repeat this process until you get the desired tiny, tiny size.

{ GOLDEN EGGS NEST RING }

DRAMATIC RINGS are all about making a statement. This project combines the beauty of nature and the drama of scale to make a big impact. It also uses a great technique for creating a semi-custom texture plate. The flower part of the ring can be used like a shadowbox to hold your favorite objects, in this case a lovely little nest.

[1]

MATERIALS

PMC3 1 pack of 45 grams
Pro Polish polishing squares
Liver of Sulfur
Aura 22

TOOLS

Basic PMC Tool Kit
Brass Brush
Rubber Tipped Clay Shaper
Needle Tool or Sharp
 Dental Tool
Ring Mandrel
Paper
Clear tape
Ping-pong ball or doming form
Selection of texture plates, brass
 or plastic
Flower shaped cookie cutter

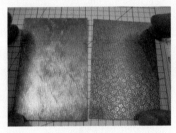

1 Select two contrasting texture plates. Use patterns that are different in scale, theme or design style.

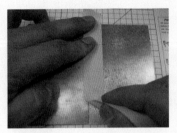

2 Tape the back of the two texture plates together. Make sure that the plates are touching tightly when the tape is adhered. If not, there will be a seam that shows when the plate is used.

3 Roll out some clay 4 cards thick, centering it over the seam of the joined texture plates.

4 Cut out the shape with a 1 1/2" flower-shaped cutter, being sure to include parts of both textures in the cutout.

5 Drape the flower over a lubricated doming form such as half of a ping-pong ball. Be sure that the texture side is face down on the form.

6 Use a brass brush to "pounce" a texture onto the back side of the flower. Set aside to dry.

7 Smooth the edges with a sanding sponge if needed. Next make a paper sleeve by wrapping a ring mandrel with a strip of paper. Secure the paper with cellophane tape, wrapping the tape all the way around the paper. The tape will create a water tight barrier.

8 The size of the ring should be approximately 2 to 2.5 times larger than your true ring size. Roll out clay 4 cards thick. Cut the clay about 1/2" wide and long enough for your size. Wrap the clay around the paper sleeve on the ring mandrel. Be sure the sleeve has been well lubricated.

9 Cut the strip of clay about 1/8" larger than needed. Cut only the top strip.

10 Using a clay shaper, smooth the seam. Set aside to dry. Remove the ring from the mandrel and slip out the paper sleeve. Smooth inside and out with sandpaper.

11 Roll out the clay 3 cards thick. Using a circle template cut out a 3/4" size circle. Form the clay over a doming form or the end of a needle tool.

12 Using a syringe, apply short lines that will make the twigs of the nest.

13 Use the wet tip of a pin tool to split the ends of the twigs and make the branches.

14 Continue adding twigs until the nest is completely built. Set aside to dry.

15 Make 3 small eggs and join them to the nest. Follow the directions on page 12 to make the eggs.

16 Join the flower structure to the ring using water and slip.

17 Join the nest to the flower using water and slip. Set aside to dry. Do any final sanding. Fire according to manufacturer's instructions. Do not polish. Add Aura 22 to the eggs and underside of the flower part of the ring. (See page 58 for the Adding Gold resource link) Finish in the usual fashion.

© *Photography by Drew Davidson*

WHAT TECHNIQUES WOULD YOU USE TO CREATE THIS PROJECT?

The materials are PMC Plus, Whimsycrete, UV Resin.

Visit www.WOODLANDCHIC.NET/MOTHERNATURE to find the answer.

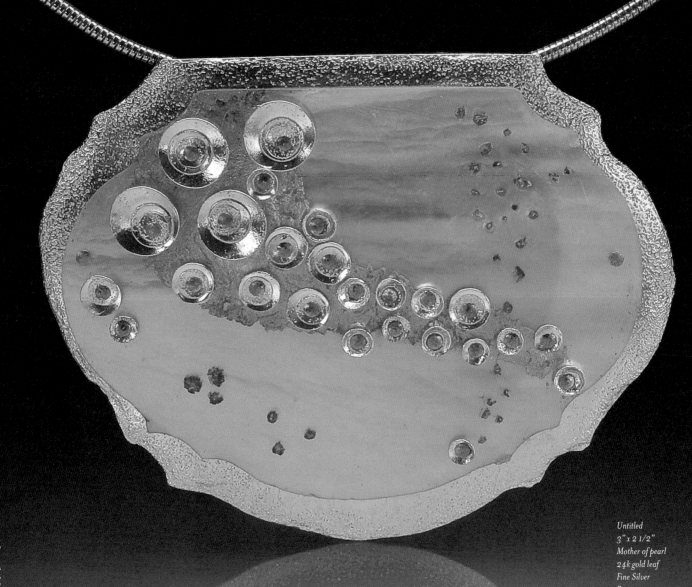

Untitled
3" x 2 1/2"
Mother of pearl
24k gold leaf
Fine Silver
Brass
Sterling Silver

PENDANT

{ LADY BUG SHRINE PENDANT }

I WAS IN THE GARDEN pruning one of my favorite rose bushes: A beautiful rose with red petals on one side and a surprise of solid white color on the underside. A lady bug landed on my garden glove. I gently placed it on a branch knowing that this little creature keeps my roses free of aphids. The perfect symbiotic relationship. This shrine pendant captures that moment in time.

[A]

MATERIALS

Elongated Shaped Rock
Rose Branch
PMC3 1 pack of 45 grams
2 Part Mold Compund
Aura 22
6" of 20 Gauge Fine Silver Wire
Paper
Trillion shaped gemstones

TOOLS

Basic Metal Clay Tool Kit
Brass Brush
Rubber Tipped Clay Shaper
Tissue Blade
Craft Knife
Flat nose pliers
Dockyard Carving Tool
   U-Gouge 1.5mm

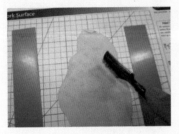

1 Roll out clay 3 cards thick. Use a brush to texture the clay or use a texture plate.

2 Gently press the clay into a mold of a rock. Cut off the excess clay with a tissue blade.

3 Set aside to dry.

4 Create the rose branch by making a mold of a branch using 2 part mold compound. Press the clay into the mold. The length of the branch should be longer than the stone.

5 Carve off the excess clay and refine the shape of the branch and thorns.

6 Cut the wire into 6 pieces that are 1/4" long. Using 2 flat nose pliers, bend the wire into the shape that will be used to make the legs.

7 Next make the body of the lady bug. Roll out one small ball shape and one egg shape.

8 Attach the two pieces together using water.

9 Use a pin tool to create a crease in the back section. This will be the wings.

10 Make small indentations with the tip of a rubber tipped clay shaper.

11 Insert the legs into the body. Next cut two 1/2" lengths of wire and ball up one end of each with a torch. These will be the antennae. Insert these into the head of the lady bug.

12 Sand the rock opening flat with sandpaper.

13 Measure the branch to fit inside the rock. Cut the branch to fit. The angle of the cut branch might need to be refined to match the angle of the inside of the rock. Attach the branch to the inside of the rock using water and paste.

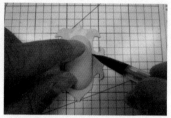

14 Download and print out the frame template at www.woodlandchic.net/frame Cut out the template. Roll out the clay 4 cards thick. Cut out the shape of the frame using a pin tool and the template. Set aside to dry. Trace the shape of the rock onto the frame.

15 Make a mark with the pencil about 1/8" inside the shape of the rock. Follow the shape of the rock all the way around. This will be the shape of the opening.

16 Create the opening by using a craft knife. Start by poking the tip into the center of the opening. Then lightly rotate the blade to cut open a hole. Next, use the craft knife to gently carve the opening to conform to the shape of the window.

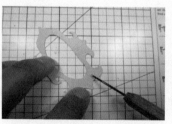

17 Use a 1.5mm U-shaped gouge to carve lines into the frame.

18 Roll tiny balls and attach them to the top and bottom of the frame using water.

19 Attach the frame to the rock using water and slip.

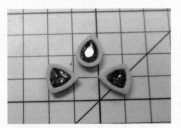

20 Set the stones in clay, dry and refine their shapes. {See page 58 for the Stone Setting resource link}

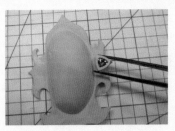

21 Attach the bezel set stones on the back of the frame using water and slip.

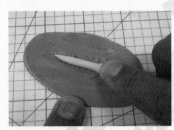

22 Make a mold of a small fern leaf. Press the clay into the mold.

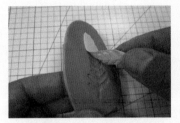

23 Lift up the clay to check the impression. Set aside to dry.

24 Connect the leaf using water.

25 Connect the lady bug to the branch using slip and water.

26 Use slip to make barbs on the legs of the lady bug. Add a drop of slip and slowly build up the layers. Fire according to manufacturer's instructions. Do not polish. Add Aura 22 to the lady bug and the inside of the rock. {See on-line resources page 56 for details of how to apply and fire Aura 22}. Torch fire, polish with brass brush and add LOS.

"Fragmented Memories Series"
1" x 1 1/2"
Fine Silver
22 K gold
Sterling Silver

This very personal series of shadowboxes explores concepts dealing with my mother's affliction with dementia. She has little nuggets of pristinely beautiful long term memories, the edges of which are slowly crumbling away.

No. 4

"A leaf fluttered in through the window this morning, as if supported by the rays of the sun, a bird settled on the fire escape, joy in the task of coffee, joy accompanied me as I walked."
~Anaïs Nin

{ FOLIAGE }

{ FOSSILIZED LEAF EARRINGS }

NATURE AT ITS BEST: Sometimes the beauty of nature commands a simple elegant solution. These fossilized earrings are as easy to make as they are beautiful. Plus, with a variety of different leaf shapes in the garden you'll never be without design options.

[B]

MATERIALS
PMC+ (or PMC3) 9 grams
2 Part Mold Compound
Ear Wires
Tiny Leaves

TOOLS
Basic PMC Tool Kit

1 Make a mold of tiny fresh picked leaves. These are grape leaves, but any leaves with prominent vein structures will do. The challenge is to find one that is small enough. Mix up the mold compound and roll it out to 8 cards thick. Position the leaves vein side toward the compound. Roll again to press the leaves in. Wait until the compound cures before removing the leaves.

2 Gather a ball of clay roughly the size of the leaf. Roll out the clay to 4 cards thick.

3 Use enough clay to push into the leaf shape. Press the excess clay into the mold leaving thin, irregular edges.

4 Check the overall shape and set aside to dry.

5 If necessary use a micro fine sanding sponge to sand the edges and back smooth.

6 Use a hand held drill to make the hole for the earring wire. Fire and finish according to manufacturer's instructions.

BRACELET
{ HINGED LEAF BRACELET }

THIS BRACELET is inspired by the botanical bracelet that I created which won 1st place in the 2007 Saul Bell Award PMC Category. With this reinterpretation of the bracelet, I have incorporated a unique and easy to make 3 hinge pin system. I've also unified each of the panels by adding a cohesive texture as a design element.

[I]

MATERIALS

PMC+ (or PMC3) 1 pack of
  45 gr and 1 pack of 28 gr
3 feet of 18 Gauge Fine Silver
  Round Wire
2" Sterling Chain
4 Jump Rings
1 Toggle Clasp

TOOLS

Basic PMC Tool Kit
Coffee Stirrer
Brass Brush
Cross Lock Tweezers
Rubber Tipped Clay Shaper
Dockyard Carving Tool
  U-Gouge 1.5mm
Butane Torch
Wire Cutters
Baking Soda
Renaissance Wax

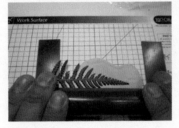

1   Roll out a lump of clay 4 cards thick. Place a lubricated leaf, vein side down, onto the clay and re-roll, pressing the leaf into the clay.

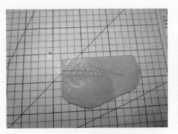

2   Remove the leaf and check the impression. Cut the panel to approximately 1 1/2" x 2 1/4". Set the rectangle-shaped panel aside to dry. Repeat for the 5 other panels.

3   Make the hinges. Roll out the clay 3 cards thick.

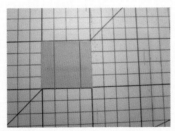

4   Cut the clay into a 1" x 1" square. Cut the square into 3 parts: 2 strips 1/4" and one strip 1/2". Each strip will be 1" long.

5   Fold each strip over a coffee stirrer and seal the edges with water. Set aside to dry on the stirrer. Repeat steps 4 and 5 three more times for a total of 4 sets of hinges.

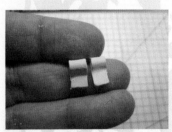

6   Gently remove the hinges from the straw. Check the inside of each hinge to ensure that it is dry. Check the size of each knuckle to be sure they are the same width.

7 Using an emery board, file each knuckle to the same width.

8 Reattach the hinges on the straw and check their movement. Make any adjustments necessary.

9 Sand each of the panels to ensure smooth edges. Using a 1.5mm U-shaped carving tool, carve small vertical lines into the background of each panel. Repeat with all panels.

10 Attach each of the hinges to the panels with water and slip. Be sure to leave at least 1/16" clearance between the hinge and the panel. Fire according to manufacturer's instructions. Use a wire brush to polish.

11 Next, using a butane torch, ball both ends of a 2" wire. Start by heating about 1/2" of wire, then concentrate the heat just above the end of the wire until it begins to melt.

12 Draw the flame up the wire and the ball will follow the flame. Repeat for the eight other wires. For the remaining 4 wires, ball only one end.

13 Insert 2 of the balled wires into the hinge. Next insert the third wire and check that the wire will not fall through the hinge. Finally, secure the end of the third wire by bending it away from the other wires and use the torch to ball the end of the wire. Double check that the wires will stay in place and not fall through the knuckle.

14 Mix up the liver of sulfur and, using a paint brush, paint the mixture onto the leaf part of each panel. Use multiple layers until you achieve the desired effect. Repeat for the other panels. Neutralize the entire bracelet in a solution of baking soda and water. Seal with Renaissance Wax.

15 Attach 1" of chain to each end of the bracelet with a jump ring. Attach toggle to one chain and toggle bar to the other.

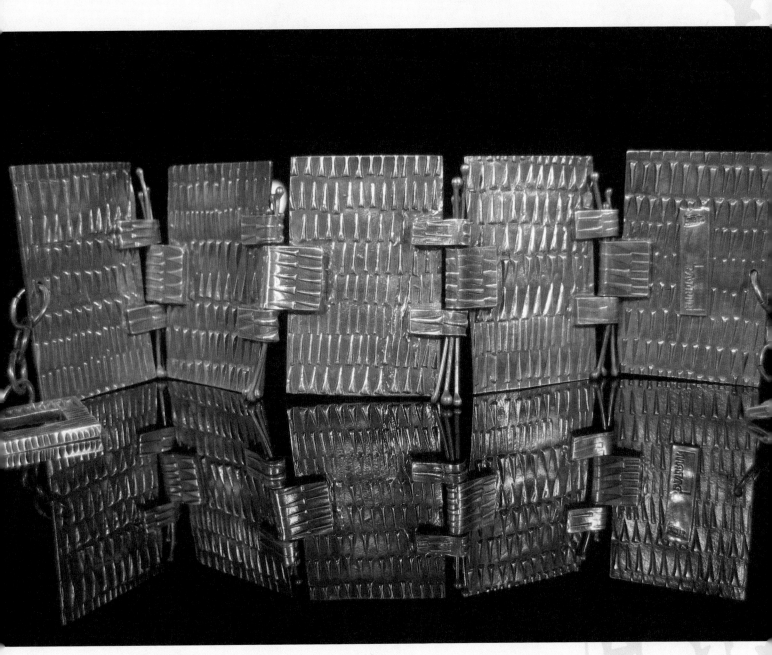

FOR AN ALTERNATIVE DESIGN ON THE BACK, WHAT TECHNIQUES WOULD YOU USE?

Visit www.WOODLANDCHIC.NET/BRACELETBACK to find the answer.

No. 5

{ FOUNDATIONS }

"Be daring, be different, be impractical, be anything that will assert integrity of purpose and imaginative vision against the play-it-safers, the creatures of the commonplace, the slaves of the ordinary."
~Cecil Beaton

{ EASY FLOWER PENDANT }

This project is perfect for those who are new to metal clay. It covers the basic steps needed to create the perfect foundation for just about any metal clay project.

[B]

MATERIALS
PMC+ (or PMC3)
1 Package 18 Grams

TOOLS
Basic PMC Tool Kit
Flower Shaped Cutter
Coffee Stirrer Straw
Butane Torch

1 Use a release agent to lubricate the texture plate and roller. Stack equal amounts of cards on top of the texture plate. Use the roller to roll the clay to an even thickness.

2 Check the clay for even thickness, even texture impression, and no bubbles.

3 Use a release agent on the cutter. Then use a cutter to cut out the flower shape. Think of how cookies are made!

4 Use a small coffee stirrer or drinking straw to cut a hole for the jump ring. Place the pendant on a teflon sheet or well lubricated playing card.

5 Dry the piece by placing it on a candle warmer or mug warmer. As an alternative you can use a food dehydrator.

6 Sand the dried pendant using the sanding sponge. Start off with the super fine grit, then progress to the micro fine.

7 Using a torch or kiln, fire the pendant according to manufacturer's instructions.

8 Use a brass brush under running water with a drop of dish soap to polish the surface.

CONNECTING METAL CLAY
The foundation of all metal clay designs hinges on 3 types of connections:

Wet-to-Wet:
To connect two pieces of wet clay. Use water at the connection to activate the binder. Hold for 3 seconds.

Dry-to-Wet:
To connect a bone dry piece of clay and a wet piece of clay. Use water on the dry piece, then press the wet clay onto the dry. Hold for 3 seconds.

Dry-to-Dry:
To connect two bone dry pieces of clay together. Wet each piece of clay with water, then use slip.

{ ON-LINE TOOLS }

Information at your fingertips. If you are new to metal clay, this is the place to start. If you are more experienced, this is the place to check out. I have included a list of PDFs for you to download with additional information on metal clay. Also included below is a list of links to videos from other parts of the book, as well as a list of templates for you to download so you can make projects in the book that require them. Please remember these resources are for your personal use only. Please do not distribute without permission. Thanks!

ON-LINE RESOURCES

Yahoo Group
http://groups.yahoo.com/
group/MetalClay

Metal Clay Academy
www.metalclayacademy.
com

Squidoo Metal Clay Lens
www.squidoo.com/
preciousmetalclay

PMC Guild
www.pmcguild.com

Art Clay Society
www.artclaysociety.com

CraftCast
www.craftcast.com

ON-LINE TOOLS
WOODLAND CHIC PDFs

Basic Tools
www.woodlandchic.net/
tools

Touch ups and repairs
www.woodlandchic.net/
repairs

Firing Options
www.woodlandchic.net/
firing

Stone Setting
www.woodlandchic.net/
stonesetting

Adding Patina
www.woodlandchic.net/
patina

Adding Gold - Aura 22
www.woodlandchic.net/
gold

WOODLAND CHIC PDFs

Faux Bois Cuff Template
www.woodlandchic.net/
cuff

Shrine Template
www.woodlandchic.net/
frame

WOODLAND CHIC VIDEOS
DESIGN CHALLENGE

Garden Gate
www.woodlandchic.net/
gardengate

Mother Nature
www.woodlandchic.net/
mothernature

Bracelet Back
www.woodlandchic.net/
braceletback

Faux Bois Bi-Metal Cuff
www.woodlandchic.net/
bimetalcuff

WOODLAND CHIC VIDEOS

How to roll a snake
www.woodlandchic.net/
snakes

Mixing Resins
www.woodlandchic.net/
resins

Firing Options
www.woodlandchic.net/
firingvideo

Mold Compound
www.woodlandchic.net/
moldcompound

Flower Swirl Pendant
www.woodlandchic.net/
pendant

Thank You
{ Acknowledgements }

My parents were not what one would consider to be the traditionally creative types. My father was in the Air Force and taught airplane electronics. My mother would these days be called a "stay at home mom"; she proudly called herself a housewife, and took care of us both. But they nurtured my every inkling for exploration of all kinds. They told me I could be anything I wanted to be, and never said no to anything I wanted to try. Well…except for when I was 12 and wanted to jump off the roof into the pool. It's this "why not try it" attitude of exploration that I carry with me to this day. It was indeed their greatest gift to me and for this I am thankful.

My journey has brought me so many influencers, people who have touched my life and help shaped me artistically. From my college years at the Fashion Institute of Design and Merchandising, instructors like Hyla Witt and Andy Ebon helped instill me with professionalism in the design world. When I worked at Macy's California Special Events Department, creative powerhouses like Larry Hashbarger and Joe Elmore opened my eyes to an all new level of creativity that turned simple hardware store finds into glorious runway fashion shows/performance art. When I attended the Academy of Art University, instructors like Paul Hogue helped me coordinate my hands with my design mind and my design eyes.

When Precious Metal Clay found it's way into my life I was so lucky to be introduced to the process by Hadar Jacobsen. I would later find out that Hadar shared my attitude of exploration. Thank you for starting me off right!

I'd also like to thank CeCe Wire whose knowledge and teaching style influences me to this very day. CeCe showed me a higher level of the art of metal clay and the fine art of making teaching look effortless.

I'm so very appreciative of my fellow metal clay artists for your words of encouragement, for allowing me to gain from your creative experience, and for accepting me into the fold so warmly. To Tim McCreight, thanks for your support in every way, from being the stellar source of information for all things metal, to your sense of humor, and for including me in all of the reindeer games. To Chris Darway and Terry Kovalcik for helping me fine tune the art of teaching a Rio certification class. To Celie Fago for taking my breath away with your stunning jewelry and showing me what can really be made with metal clay. To Barbara Becker Simon for your friendship and creative support and encouragement, both on the road and over the internet. To Tonya Davidson for allowing my creative muse to play with yours. To Jeanette Landenwitch and CeCe Wire for leading our metal clay community and spreading the word about this fabulous material.

I'd also like to acknowledge my friends at Rio Grande who took me into their family so warmly. Alan Bell, Kevin Whitmore, Gail Philippi, Virginia Dickson, Yvonne Padilla, and Nate Perea, thanks for your support, knowledge and hours of work to make the community of metal clay a more knowledge-able place! My students and I are grateful.

To my friends at Aftosa, Arnie and Jerilyn, who have been both generous and supportive of my work, and for their support for the metal clay community. Thanks to the talents of Abby Johnston and Drew Davidson, whose additional photography, as noted, made such a glamorous addition to the book. Many thanks to Pat Evans who kept my grammar on track in all of "it's" glory, thanks for editing "Woodland Chic" both technically and grammatically. An extra special thanks to Jenn Zahrt, Vielen dank für ihre liebe zum detail! I hope google translate made a sentence *you* can read because I sure can't!!

I'd also love to acknowledge my wonderful, talented, enthusiastic students around the country who encouraged me to write this book. You guys rock! I appreciate your passion, it fuels me.

A special thanks to Paulette Traverso, who's the only person who would realize that pigeon feet would be an appropriate gift. Your friendship and creativity mean the world to me.

Last but not least, I'd like to acknowledge the support of my life partner Steven Warrick who is my rock. Without your support and understanding, this book would not happen. Thanks for putting up with my late nights in the studio, searching for the "lost project," and for being the kind, supportive and non-judgemental soul that you are. I'm lucky to have you in my life.

{ ABOUT THE AUTHOR }

VISIT
WWW.PATRIKSSTUDIO.COM
FOR MORE INFORMATION
AND CLASSES.

Patrik's unique vision for his jewelry designs has won praise from jewelry collectors both nationally and internationally. His experience in the worlds of design and fashion helped shape his creative vision and brand. He is a graduate of the Fashion Institute of Design and Merchandising and The Academy of Art University. He worked as a Fashion Stylist at Macy's San Francisco and was the owner and Creative Director of Wallop Design Group, a graphic design and branding company.

He is currently pursuing his passion as a jewelry artist and instructor. He teaches metal clay workshops in the San Francisco Bay Area and nationally. Patrik is a member of the PMC Guild and is both PMC Guild Certified and Art Clay Certified. He is one of 10 senior instructors for Rio Grande and teaches PMC certification workshops nationwide. He was a featured artist on HGTV's "That's Clever." Patrik's work has been published in numerous books and publications such as *500 Pendants and Lockets* by Lark Books, *New Directions in Metal Clay: 25 Creative Jewelry Projects* by CeCe Wire, Lapidary Journal and *MJSA Journal*, among others. He has written articles for *Art Jewelry Magazine* both on-line and in print, *Metal Clay Artist Magazine* and has authored numerous tutorials for Whole Lotta Whimsy, Aftosa, Rio Grande and CraftCast.com. He is also the recipient of the 2007 Saul Bell Award 1st place in PMC.

*This pendant has a several techniques that are perfect for beginning and intermediate level students. You'll learn how to make a pendant with dimension by using a doming form. You'll also lean how to roll a snake. Visit www.woodland.net/pendant

Printed in Great Britain
by Amazon.co.uk, Ltd.,
Marston Gate.